STARTACULAR
TRAINING IN THE ART OF INITIATIVE

DANIEL ZOLLER

VESUVIUS PUBLISHING LLC
921 EAST DUPONT ROAD, SUITE 789
FORT WAYNE, IN 46825

COPYRIGHT © 2013 BY DANIEL ZOLLER

COVER CREATED BY SEBASTIAN DIEZ

ALL RIGHTS RESERVED

For my mother, Julie

"I know of no more encouraging fact than the unquestionable ability of man to elevate his life by conscious endeavor."

— Henry David Thoreau

CONTENTS

Introduction...1

Part One: The Case for Initiative.....................4

1. Failures of action................................5
2. Indispensable action............................17
3. Initiative is action personified................29
4. The versatile power of initiative..............38

Part Two: How to Build Initiative...............46

1. Blueprint...47
2. Judge your efforts by how well you start....56
3. Start without hesitation.......................71
4. Practice small action...........................90
5. Start again, relentlessly.....................104
6. Adopt action as a value......................118

INTRODUCTION

For most people, action is a liability, an opportunity to fail. As in, *If you don't study enough for this test, you're going to fail. Fix your resume, or you won't get any interviews. If you don't try harder, you're never going to lose that weight.* These are clear messages about the role of action in our lives: *Do your work or you'll be sorry.*

And maybe our perception of action as a threat and a risk—something to screw up—is justified; after all, we *do* fail for lack of effort—a lot. We develop a negative relationship with action through disappointing experiences, all those times we let ourselves down.

This book teaches you how to transform action from a liability into an asset, from a threat into a weapon. It teaches you how to build *initiative* by becoming an effective starter.

As you'll see, persistent starting is the most obvious secret of productivity. It's easy to understand *why* people of great initiative, people who *just keep going*, often meet with tremendous success. The universe is happy to reward those who strive in earnest. But for many of us, the questions of *how* to build persistence, *how* to start without hesitation, and *how* to become great at taking action have remained unanswered.

In *Startacular*, you will find practical and specific techniques for approaching any goal with initiative. You'll learn exactly how to defeat procrastination and start without hesitation, how to make rapid and comfortable progress through short, focused bursts of effort, and how to be relentless in starting again.

You'll also finish with a better appreciation for the power of sustained action, and how to ensure that personal initiative is the principal creative force in your life. As you develop skill through intelligent practice, action will become a powerful engine to drive all your ambitions.

PART ONE: THE CASE FOR INITIATIVE

1. FAILURES OF ACTION

"Defeat is not the worst of failures. Not to have tried is the true failure."

— George Edward Woodbury

LIFE'S RAINBOW OF FAILURES

The catalog of human failures is robust. When someone can't resist smoking cigarettes, that's a failure of willpower. If you can't find the money to go on vacation, it's a failure of resources. A failure of judgment finds you sleeping with your boss's spouse. And failures of planning and discretion get you caught (and fired).

Given the many paths to failure, it's no surprise that so often things just don't turn out. Marriages fail to last. My team fails to reach the finals. Your teenage son fails to convince the police that weed isn't his. We're imperfect creatures, and early on we learn to accept that failure is part of life.

But today we're scratching a deep line in the dirt of failure. That's because there is one class of failure so destructive, so ugly and embarrassing, that it must be unmasked and destroyed if we're to have any hope of fulfilling our life's potential: the failure to act.

FAILURES OF ACTION

"And we are now men, and must accept in the highest mind the same transcendent destiny; and not minors and invalids in a protected corner, not cowards fleeing before a revolution, but guides, redeemers, and benefactors, obeying the Almighty effort, and advancing on Chaos and the Dark." — Ralph Waldo Emerson, *Self-Reliance*

A failure of action occurs every time you don't do what you know you ought to do. You turn your back on opportunity, give up on something useful before you can make progress, or drag your feet instead of charging ahead with your ambitions.

We're not talking about giving it everything you've got and falling short. You and I both know there's no shame in that. A thorough but unsuccessful effort can often transform itself into renewed commitment, better plans, or a fresh start. But there is a canyon of difference between not accomplishing something and *not doing it*.

There is no need to split hairs about what constitutes a thorough effort. You know when you've done the work. And you *feel*, even more acutely, when you've been the coward fleeing before your own revolution. "But God," Emerson warned, "will not have his work made manifest by cowards."

THE FOUR HORSEMEN OF INACTION

We can trace all failures of action back to one or more of these behaviors:

- Doing nothing (avoidance)
- Chronic delay or hesitation (procrastination)
- Quitting early (abandonment)
- Weak, inconsistent or inadequate effort (insufficiency)

This list is given in no particular order, because each of these behaviors have equal power to block your growth. In terms of output, an insufficient effort is no worse than doing nothing at all—both yield nothing. Wait too long or give up too soon, it makes no difference. All failures of action are complete. If they weren't, they would be small or large successes.

THE SADDEST FAILURE

"Misfortunes one can endure—they come from the outside, they are accidents. But to suffer for one's own faults—there is the sting of life!" — Oscar Wilde

Failures of action are the saddest of all failures. They only happen when we don't exercise control in one of the few areas of life where we *actually have control*: what we do with our energy, our intellect, and the days we've been given.

It's a sobering thought. The bad breaks and uphill battles of life make it hard enough to thrive without adding self-sabotage to the mix; understanding this, it's truly pitiful when we just can't be bothered to take action in our own best interest.

THE YESTERDAY TEST

"This is the first lesson to learn. Be determined not to curse anything outside, not to lay blame upon anyone outside, but stand up, lay the blame on yourself. You will find that is always true. Get hold of yourself." — Swami Vivekananda

I'm sometimes approached by my undergraduate business students seeking job-hunting tips. By the time they come to me, they are typically in a panic. It's quite difficult for students and recent graduates to secure desirable internships and full-time positions in the current (read: shitty) job market.

I listen as they explain that nobody wants to hire someone without experience right now (*but how am I supposed to get experience without a job?*), that you have to know somebody to get a good job, and how the deck is both generally and specifically stacked against them.

I don't necessarily disagree with their complaints. The job market can be a carnival of horrors for a newly minted graduate. But I always reply the same way, by asking:

"What did you do about it yesterday?"

Now I receive a look of impatient confusion, like I hadn't listened to what they just said. So I clarify: "Tell me what you did yesterday to try and get a good job. What steps did you take, specifically?" When I first employed this question, my intent was to understand the student's daily job-hunting tactics, so I could try to help them improve their methods.

But nine times out of ten, their honest answer is "nothing". Outside of the university's structured but limited career services program, they aren't really doing much besides worrying. And that just isn't enough to justify any complaining or self-pity.

The 'yesterday' test applies remarkably well in many contexts, and it almost always unmasks a failure of action. From weight loss to job hunting to artistic pursuits, *most* failures must be judged as failures of action. Why? If you can't pass a survey of your daily efforts, obviously you are the problem.

But the standard of guilt for a failure of action is actually much lower. If you can't absolve yourself as a *potential* culprit (that is, if you haven't yet done *everything* you can), you must assume that you *are* the culprit. To assign blame outside yourself would require a rather suspect and cowardly logic.

Until you've exhausted yourself doing everything in your power to achieve your end, the blame for any failure lies with you.

GOOD NEWS

The failure of action's most humiliating qualities—*you* don't give the effort, *you* don't take control, and so *you* are solely to blame—are also its most encouraging. They promise us that failures of action may be wholly avoided, simply by taking adequate action when you should. No one but yourself can stop you.

To be sure, eliminating failures of action won't guarantee success. Nothing guarantees success. You might ultimately fail some other way, due to circumstances you can't control. You might fail because you do your best and it's not good enough. Competitive athletes, for example, know better than most that you can give a complete effort and still get beat. That's life. If you don't want to play, go home.

But if you're willing to throw yourself into the

fray, know that you don't ever have to die by your own sword—you don't ever have to fail for lack of effort. Eliminating failures of action will bring you a great deal of peace. It's much easier to accept inevitable setbacks and disappointments with a clear conscience, with no regrets, knowing you've done your part.

More importantly, committing to action as a *modus operandi* is possibly the single best step you can take to ensure a degree of success in life; this truth applies to every type of goal. For success, sustained effort is not optional. As we'll see, taking action is the vital spark required to realize your potential.

2. INDISPENSABLE ACTION

"Action may not always bring happiness, but there is no happiness without action."

— Benjamin Disraeli

ACTION IS MAGIC (AN ODE TO ACTION)

Action is a charming devil. Improvement and progress follow action around like shadows. Success looks up to action like an older brother, and constantly endeavors to win action's favor. Mastery offers itself freely to action because mastery owes action everything.

Action breeds satisfaction and builds skill. Action is a savior to the depressed. Action quiets a restless mind. Action steadies when confidence wavers. Action teaches and action learns; action reveals the true nature of things. Action has a way of producing unforeseen and critical assistance when we most need it.

The universe lavishes its rewards on action because action—growth, change, movement—is no less than the essence of life itself. To embrace action is to ally yourself with the motive force of all creation.

WHY WE SNUB ACTION

It's curious that despite action's royal status among its peers (success, progress, mastery etc.), many of us treat action more like a dusty relic. You mean I just *get started*? Focus on doing useful things each day, little by little, until it pays off? How *passé*. Any idiot could do that.

In the age of the shortcut, the secret hack and the quick fix, it seems that action doesn't stand a chance of winning our affections. First, action is simple. How could something so obvious, something freely and equally available to everyone, possibly be effective? Second, sustained and persistent action means real work—taking action *is* work—and work typically isn't the answer people are looking for.

Try telling a fresh-faced art student or aspiring writer that the single means of unlocking their unique creative genius is putting in the hours, doing the work no matter what. Watch their eyes glaze over as they look around for someone else to talk to. Try suggesting to a friend that their fitness program is failing because they don't really exercise all that much. That's the last time they ask *you* for advice.

Action also gets snubbed because we're more attracted to, and distracted by, a host of fashionable newcomers: positive thinking and affirmations, mentoring, time management, minimalism and the rest. These techniques are pushed as cure-alls for personal development, but do not mistake what is only helpful for that which is truly essential.

FALSE IDOLS OF PRODUCTIVITY

Make a game of critically evaluating any theories of personal development you come across. Under scrutiny, most self-help tenets prove to be more suggestion than rule.

Do you believe, for example, that positive thinking, support and encouragement are prerequisites for success?

Legendary writer/director Woody Allen swears he has "never been satisfied or even pleased" with a single film he's made, yet his work is popular and his output is prolific (Allen releases a new film almost every year).

Vincent van Gogh changed art forever with his dynamic, energetic paintings featuring thick, aggressive brushstrokes. His style was unusual, and he endured a steady flood of criticism and discouragement from people whose opinions he respected and whose approval he craved. Among them were close family members and fellow artists. Many times they hinted that Vincent should give it up; sometimes they were more explicit, literally begging him to stop painting.

But van Gogh worked with almost superhuman energy and commitment. He often woke before dawn to prepare his materials, and stopped painting only when it was too dark to see. Today he endures as one of history's most recognizable and beloved artists. Positivity and encouragement are fine, but they're not essential.

Maybe you've heard that to become great you must specialize and maintain a very narrow focus.

Leonardo da Vinci was spectacularly productive in so many fields—art, mechanical engineering, architecture, anatomy, the natural sciences and writing, among others—that a new term was coined to describe someone so versatile—the

"Renaissance man". Cynics might argue that such a career has become impossible due to an ever-increasing pressure to specialize. If that's true, then it's hard to explain the accomplishments of a modern Renaissance man like Steve Martin, an acclaimed actor, comedian, novelist, playwright, producer and musician.

Try repeating this exercise in healthy skepticism, using the following elements sometimes touted as 'necessary' for achievement:

Efficiency
Emphasis on process over outcome
Present-moment focus
Deliberate practice
Clear, fixed goals
Time management
Organization
People skills
Strong health and high energy
Prioritization
Patience

Self-discipline
Solitude
Optimism
Coaching and mentoring
Passion
Intelligence
Access to resources (money, connections etc.)
Talent

With a little curiosity (and maybe some research), you can find notable exceptions to most of the so-called keys to success.

Please don't misunderstand this criticism. The existence of exceptions doesn't disprove the overall utility of a concept or practice. Sensible techniques can and do improve results when combined with persistent action and a decent plan. But none of the items listed above represent the silver bullet we so naturally crave. None of them are *absolutely necessary*.

But what, you ask, is the harm in exploring various techniques if they can help?

TINKERING

"Isn't it the height of folly to learn inessential things when time is so desperately short!"
— Seneca

To emphasize supporting or complementary techniques before mastering what is essential is a bit like focusing on being distracted.

Imagine you wish to become a better golfer. You might lower your scores slightly by purchasing better equipment, studying course design and strategy, or by playing to your weaknesses (aiming shots far left to accommodate a nasty slice, for example).

Temporary improvement can often be secured by such patchwork fixes. But you will *never* be an exceptional golfer unless you develop an effective, reliable golf swing. Improvement by any other means is mere tinkering and will not produce lasting results. The swing is the one indispensable element in golf.

The same principle applies to achievement and failures of action. You will never solve failures of action by any means other than action. If you want to stop wasting time and start producing, you must first understand and embrace this fact: for achievement in any endeavor, persistent action is the one indispensable element.

THE ONE INDISPENSABLE ELEMENT OF ACHIEVEMENT

You will never read this: "The achievements of _____ are particularly remarkable, because he found it very difficult to get started and worked toward his most important goals rarely and inconsistently, if at all."

Action is not optional or negotiable. Every undertaking demands it as a minimum, the price of opportunity. If you won't pay, you won't move. Sometimes action isn't all that's required, but *action is always required.*

And many times, to our surprise and delight, action by itself *is* enough. Even when other advantages are missing, action lands with titanic force against resistance, and overwhelms the defenses of circumstance. That's why people of modest abilities and humble means often rise to great heights. Initiative charges through history as the Great Equalizer.

The reverse, however, never occurs. Ambitious idlers create nothing. Gifted procrastinators wait themselves to death. Success always rejects the lazy and passive man, regardless of opportunity or ability. "Nothing," Calvin Coolidge observed, "is more common than unsuccessful people with talent… unrewarded genius is almost a proverb." The duty of sustained action stands between mediocrity and greatness as an uncompromising gatekeeper.

Without persistent, sustained effort nothing gets done, nothing advances. Even those accomplishments which appear more like *non-doing*, such as obtaining a quiet mind through meditation, require sustained practice and persistent starting. In short, wherever we find achievement, action was there first, as the vital spark.

3. INITIATIVE IS ACTION PERSONIFIED

"They always say time changes things, but you actually have to change them yourself."

— Andy Warhol

INITIATIVE IS A SKILL

Initiative is a trait we ascribe to people who take action; initiative is action personified. We easily recognize this trait in others. They stand out because of what they *do*. They get started before everyone else. They rarely make excuses, and seem to prefer just getting down to it. Action is their *modus operandi*. People of initiative often seem like forces of nature. They carry an air of confidence and possibility.

If you needed to pick someone with initiative for a team, you would probably articulate a standard rooted in observable behaviors, and then look for someone whose work patterns match the profile. Such a process reveals a very functional view of initiative.

But something odd happens when we think of initiative in relation to our own lives. It becomes a sort of fantastic ideal, removed from any practical context or application. Phrases like "*Go confidently in the direction of your dreams!*" make our hearts race. Imagining the richness of life as someone who acts decisively and without hesitation provides a certain guilty pleasure.

But those are only abstractions. To understand the distinction, consider another trait: strength. There is strength as an abstraction (*e.g.* "strength in numbers"), and then there is strength as a real ability that can be observed, measured and enhanced (as happens in weight lifting).

To harness initiative for daily use and profit (the purpose of this book), we must stop thinking of it as an abstraction or a credential awarded in hindsight. We must recognize initiative as a concrete behavior and a living, breathing skill.

TWO TYPES OF INITIATIVE

The kind of concrete initiative we're after shows up *every day*. Once established, it becomes a defining quality of your work and a part of your personality. These traits separate *true initiative* from *incidental initiative*, which is equally useful but totally unreliable.

Incidental initiative arrives to accommodate a burst of inspiration, a surge in motivation, an emergency or a looming deadline. It flares up fast and burns out quickly. That's because incidental initiative is reactive; it relies on external stimulus. When the stimulus resolves or grows stale, incidental initiative disappears. The research paper is finished. The wedding is over. Oil painting wasn't as easy or fun as it looked. You're right back to passive, idle and disengaged.

True initiative is proactive and ongoing, a weapon

you can deploy in every task. True initiative drives you forward at the very moment things become difficult or uncomfortable. Instead of relaxing or sighing relief, true initiative feeds on the adrenaline of progress, and remains ever-eager to attack your Next Big Scheme.

A SIMPLE STANDARD

So who qualifies as a person of true initiative, a person who lives and breathes action? How do you know when you've got it? We don't want a complicated or pedantic definition. Initiative manifests itself in a variety of experiences and circumstances, and our standard should embrace the entire range. We're going to adopt one that's both simple and definite.

People of initiative are always eager to get started, and they're good at it. They enjoy taking action, and find sustaining motivation in their own efforts.

It's most accurate to think of initiative as a combination of 1) skill and 2) inclination. However this is not a hard distinction; skill and inclination push and reinforce one another in a productive spiral.

With enhanced skill comes increased inclination (to use the skill), and growing inclination leads to further practice and even greater skill. As you improve at starting and taking action, you'll become more interested in using those abilities.

INITIATIVE IS YOUR NATURE

Like all skills, initiative must be developed through concentrated practice. And that's a bit of a shame, because everyone is born with tremendous initiative. Children learn about the world around them primarily through incessant, enthusiastic exploration. For a child, action is a way of life.

Young children naturally go after whatever they want, without hesitation. They must be *trained* to exercise restraint or ask for permission. Thanks to years of socializing, childhood initiative atrophies and eventually dies on our way into young adulthood. To best fit in, we learn to value caution, analysis and conformity over boldness and action, which are often seen as risky.

That is not to say childlike initiative is a desirable quality in an adult. Patience and discretion do have value, and you won't gain much by regressing to childish impulsiveness (*What happens if I touch this hot stove*?). I only mean to point out that initiative is your *original state*, your inheritance at birth. Energized, decisive action comes naturally to us all. Passive hesitation, on the other hand, is a learned behavior. It's great for laying low and blending in, but useless for creating an exceptional life.

When you develop initiative, then, you are not adopting a forced attitude or some special way of doing things. You are embracing the most natural inclinations of your curious, ambitious mind, and leveraging the uniquely human capacity for forward-thinking, creative action.

4. THE VERSATILE POWER OF INITIATIVE

"Teach a man to fish and you feed him for a lifetime."

— Chinese proverb

INITIATIVE TRAINING WILL HELP YOU MAKE REAL PROGRESS NOW

By now you should understand why action is an absolute requirement for achievement. Without persistent effort, your plans are doomed to fail. If you won't do the work, your dreams are already dead. To these truths there are no exceptions.

You also know that to possess initiative is to be good at taking action, and that initiative is a skill you can develop with practice. But initiative is not a secondary or complementary skill to work on in your spare time. Practicing initiative is the single best way to make progress and get things done. Action is movement, and initiative training will improve your results right away.

That's because initiative is a meta-skill (a skill which creates value when applied to other skills) and cannot be practiced directly. You must develop initiative by practicing it on something. Painting is learned by painting, and singing is learned by singing, but initiative is learned by doing. This flexibility—*doing* is the thing being practiced—means you can choose *anything worth doing* to serve as a vehicle for practicing initiative. For example, initiative could be developed through painting, singing, or both.

To apply the advice contained in the second part of this book, you will choose a vehicle—some personal task, project or goal. As you train yourself to work with initiative toward your goal, you will make real and rapid progress. This doubles the value of initiative training; see it as an opportunity to develop a useful skill while making progress on something important. Whatever your ambition, learning how to pursue it with initiative is the best way to start.

Once learned, initiative is a versatile skill with broad utility. Consider these three powerful qualities of initiative:

INITIATIVE IS INFRASTRUCTURE

Infrastructure consists of the foundations which support or enable a larger system. Infrastructure establishes the frame and smoothes the way. Railroads, indoor plumbing, and wired electricity are familiar examples. We typically don't think much about infrastructure. It hums along thanklessly in the background as we go about our lives. But when infrastructure is broken or missing, everything grinds to a halt, and we can think of nothing else.

Reliable initiative provides infrastructure to support your efforts. When you're working effectively, you don't think about how or when to get started. You are focused on the challenges of your task. But shaky initiative undermines your system and consumes attention that could be applied to something useful. If you have trouble starting, things break down quickly. Like a fallen bridge stops traffic, difficulty in getting started blocks progress.

With training, however, you can turn reliable initiative (your ability and inclination to get down to work without hesitation, whenever the opportunity presents itself) into an enabling foundation, an advantage, and one less thing to worry about. You won't lose time to procrastination or indecision. Working with initiative will lead you to uncommon and interesting progress.

INITIATIVE IS VERSATILE

Athletic talents like explosive speed and exceptional coordination are universally valuable; they enhance an athlete's potential in any sport. And initiative, like intelligence or sound judgment, invariably increases performance in our personal pursuits.

If you are diligent, initiative training will make you a reliable starter and an effective doer. You will possess a powerful engine of activity and output. Once built, this engine can be run on any track—you can apply a robust initiative to everything you do. Think of it as a giant Swiss army knife in your productivity toolbox. As an adaptable and versatile skill, initiative brings every type of goal closer within reach.

INITIATIVE IS A SKILL MULTIPLIER

Kids play a game where a genie grants you a single wish. The clever kids always figure out that the best wish is to ask for more wishes (duh). Like a wish for more wishes, initiative is a skill that builds other skills. Initiative is a skill multiplier.

When you're learning something new, the most important thing is consistent practice and exposure. But practice can be boring. People don't usually give up on a new skill for lack of progress. They give up because the progress they do make is irregular and incremental. Most people lose interest when they reach a plateau and no further breakthrough is in sight. Of course, it's impossible to perfect a skill without enduring those plateaus, which can last for weeks or months.

But someone with strong initiative respects practice and isn't afraid to grind, even without the promise of immediate improvement. They value action for action's sake, and don't require constant progress to sustain motivation. They work calmly with the knowledge that, eventually, all skills yield to persistence.

For devoted starters, skill acquisition can also be a source of great pleasure. Because they pride themselves on making an effort, the process of applying themselves to something can be as rewarding as any instrumental gains.

People of initiative also savor the intellectual challenge of taming a new skill, of breaking it down into actionable pieces that can be studied, mastered and recombined. When their enthusiasm for an activity fluctuates (as it must), they don't indulge in self-defeating debates about whether they should keep going. They're too busy figuring out how to solve the puzzle, and having a good time doing it.

PART TWO: HOW TO BUILD INITIATIVE

1. BLUEPRINT

"The world is ready to give up its secrets if we only know how to knock, how to give it the necessary blow."

— Swami Vivekananda

JUMP START YOUR PROGRESS
AND ELIMINATE FAILURES OF ACTION

You don't have to let inaction derail any more of your plans. You can free yourself from the demoralizing guilt of could have, should have and didn't. It's possible to completely eliminate failures of action, by approaching everything you do with initiative. The second part of this book teaches you exactly how to build that initiative by practicing persistent, energized action.

First, you will learn a simple method for tracking your starts, and why you should measure success by how well (and how often) you get started.

Next, you will learn to:

- Eliminate hesitation and make starting easier
- Use short bursts of focused effort so that taking action is natural and enjoyable

- Stop without guilt, regardless of your progress
- Find and seize opportunities to start again

Finally, you will infuse these methods with emotional commitment by adopting action as a cherished value.

With daily practice, these techniques will jump start your progress on any goal, quickly generating powerful momentum. Together they also form an effective, proactive workflow which can guide your efforts over time. As you gain experience with the process and enjoy success, taking immediate and productive action will become your preferred approach to anything.

NOT THE 'ACTION HABIT'

The word *habit* hasn't appeared in this book until now. The omission was deliberate. It would be easy to insist that you "build the action habit" or "make a habit of taking initiative". But both would be misleading, and the reasons why are important. If you understand the limitations of habits and habit-building, you can better appreciate the true spirit of initiative.

Study definitions of *habit* and you'll see words like *involuntary* and *automatic*. Habits are unconscious action; do a certain thing a certain way enough times and it becomes an impulse. Consider the habit of brushing your teeth. The experience never changes—you perform the same motions at the same time every day. Teeth brushing happens on auto-pilot, and that's for the best. You would gain nothing by contemplating if, when or how you should brush your teeth. Habits are great when it's best to hand over the reins, when nothing more than mindless repetition is required. Set it and forget it.

But mindless, inflexible repetition is also a major limitation. Building a new habit relies on the erosion of discretion and creative engagement as you train mind and body to repeat a pattern over and over, without variation. And once built, a habit cannot be applied beyond its programming, nor can it be transferred to a different activity. Brushing your teeth each morning and night for 43 years will not help you build the discipline to lose weight or learn a new language in year 44.

There is nothing automatic or involuntary about initiative. Initiative is a dynamic skill and a mindset, not a rigid habit. Attacking a goal with initiative is a *conscious* process; it requires agility, flexibility and creativity.

As you practice the techniques described in coming chapters—many of which could be classed as habits—strive to remain fully engaged. Never run on auto-pilot. A person of initiative develops useful habits, but does not rely on them. She always pursues her task with imagination and awareness. She freely adapts her efforts to avoid stalling, stopping or quitting. She practices a sort of guerrilla productivity, and secures momentum and progress by any means necessary. This is the spirit of initiative.

CHOOSE A VEHICLE

Remember that you cannot practice initiative directly; it's an applied skill and you need to use it on something. The techniques here in Part Two can be applied to anything. They will help you find a job, write a book, clean out the garage, learn to play tennis or start a charity. Everything can be done with initiative.

However, for now I recommend that you choose one goal or activity to serve as your primary vehicle for developing initiative. Mastering each technique requires consistency, and it's easier when you have something to focus on. So choose a vehicle, and commit to following the prescribed techniques in all your efforts related to that activity.

Focused practice will quickly prove to you that approaching your chosen goal with initiative yields dramatic results. That experience will give you confidence to use the same methods in every pursuit, knowing they'll deliver.

You may already have a vehicle chosen. Perhaps an urgent project or neglected labor of love attracted you to this book. If so, use that. If you're flexible, consider the following guidelines:

Choose something important to you. It's absolutely essential that you choose something you're willing to invest in.

Choose something useful. If you want to become great at playing video games, you don't need initiative. You can rely on addiction.

Choose actions, not omissions. It's difficult to strengthen your initiative by working on something that mostly requires omissions (*e.g.* quitting smoking).

Don't choose a single habit. As explained in the previous chapter, initiative is a dynamic engine. Habit is a programmed response. For example, waking up at six a.m. every day won't build initiative; it only requires sufficient, unchanging repetition. But why do you want to get up so early? To work in your garden? Then make gardening your vehicle.

Choose something you're free to do. Your vehicle should be something you have control over, with nothing standing in the way of making a start. Rock band practice requires the availability and participation of every other band member, so it's not an ideal choice for developing *your* initiative. Songwriting or learning a new instrument, on the other hand, would be perfect.

2. JUDGE YOUR EFFORTS BY HOW WELL YOU START

"A man is rich in proportion to the number of things which he can afford to let alone."

— Henry David Thoreau

FOCUS ON STARTING

From here on out, we're going to cultivate a healthy obsession with starting.

Not Starting with a capital "S"—doing something new for the first time—but rather tiny, repetitive starting. Starting and stopping and starting again.

Starting with an S is nothing more than a shot of adrenaline. It's also a popular excuse to buy a new laptop or fancier gym clothes. Like a holiday firework, the shine of a Grand First Gesture begins to fade even as it bursts. New beginnings are mostly an exercise in self-congratulation, which explains their wild popularity. We make a vow, swear an oath, and the whole thing feels great.

But anything that ultimately gets done is a result of all the little starts that come after those shallow photo opportunities. The little starts, then, must become your obsession. Working with initiative means starting and starting again. Starting is the heart of initiative. Unless and until you become an effective starter, you haven't got it. But if you can master starting, you will be hard to stop.

It's obvious that what doesn't get started can never be finished, and that all completed efforts are a collection of starts. Effective starters sometimes fail, but non-starters never succeed. That is the logician's proof for the necessity of starting. But why a focus on starting? Why prioritize starting to the exclusion of everything else?

STARTING IS THE HARDEST PART OF DOING

"There's a secret that real writers know that wannabe writers don't, and the secret is this: It's not the writing part that's hard. What's hard is sitting down to write." — Steven Pressfield, *The War of Art*

Most of what we consider hard to do is actually just hard to start. Take running, for example. All you have to do is move fast enough that nobody would accuse you of walking. Running isn't hard. But getting off your ass, out of the house, and into the street to run is very hard. The first fifty yards from your doorstep to the end of the block present a greater obstacle than all the distance you'll cover after you round that corner.

But why should starting be so hard? In most cases, work you do in the first few minutes isn't much different from the work you are doing an hour later. The answer is momentum. Consider that a jumbo jet uses about 5,000 gallons of fuel (10 percent of its total capacity) during takeoff, which lasts less than a minute. Sitting on the ground with no momentum, gravity and dense low-altitude air drag against the craft and hold it back.

But after that tremendous initial burst, remaining airborne is much easier in terms of energy use. We humans fight against the initial drag of work, too. The first few minutes are often the most uncomfortable, and many times we don't make it off the ground.

Starting is the hardest part of doing. If you want to be an effective doer, you must become a reliable starter.

FOCUSING ON THE FINISH
ISN'T EFFECTIVE

Steve Jobs said "real artists ship." Meaning if you don't have output, you don't have much. And that's true in a basic way. Progress is important, both as a source of feedback and motivation. But a focus on the finish can backfire, especially in the early and middle stages of a project or goal; it actually makes finishing more difficult and less likely. It pushes the target far away, to a distance where your reach exceeds your grasp.

Try walking down a city street with your head up and your eyes fixed firmly on the horizon (the most distant point you can see). You won't get far without looking down; your brain demands quality information about your immediate surroundings, because that's where your body is. To reach the horizon, you have to navigate the terrain just in front of you. Focusing on the next step is always the fastest way to move forward.

The next step is also the next start, and that's where your project or goal is *now*. If you want to finish things, focus on starting them, again and again.

And what about all those things that just *cannot be finished*? You can never declare your house forever clean. You cannot become permanently fit. Each requires ongoing maintenance and perpetual effort. Someone with an impatient, 'are we there yet?' mindset is ill-equipped to excel at long-term pursuits. But one who focuses their energy on starting with consistency won't have any trouble making gains or keeping them.

So how exactly should you focus on starting? You keep track of your starts, adopt starting as your one metric for performance, and stop worrying about everything else.

TRACK YOUR STARTS

Data is your friend. As the sayings go, what can be measured can be improved, and what gets measured gets managed. So begin paying close attention to your starts, and make a habit of writing them down. A small notebook is all you need. Here's how I format mine:

Friday, January 4th

START   8:03
STOP   8:50
START   2:15
STOP   2:36
START   4:00
STOP   4:10
START   4:25
STOP   5:50

I fill out a page like this each day to track my

writing. Even when I'm working a lot, this process requires less than 10 minutes total. I keep it really simple so that it won't become a burden and make me want to ditch the habit—the data is too valuable.

You can see that the entries are very specific. I never round times up or down, and I never estimate. I note the START time right before I open my word processor, and I seal each entry with a STOP time just as I get up to do something else. Sometimes I make a note of how many words I wrote during each session, but not always. The starting data is what I'm after.

Tracking starts creates the awareness you can build change upon. After a few days you'll know how much time you are really committing to something. Usually it's far less than you believed, because your mental accounting probably includes all the time you spend *thinking* about your task while doing other things. Without the tracking to keep me honest, I would have declared that I spent the day of January 4th writing. The reality: I wrote for two hours and forty three minutes.

Blind to reality, you too will overestimate your efforts and not ask yourself: Am I doing as much as I can, as much as I should, as much as I want to be doing? You cannot close the gap between ambition and reality until you know reality.

MAKE STARTING YOUR ONE METRIC FOR PERFORMANCE

The objective data collected by tracking starts will support your efforts, but the *subjective importance* you give to starting is the emotional foundation of a focus on starting. After all, something you measure but do not care about is meaningless. You must begin to care deeply about how well and how often you get started, and judge your efforts on that basis.

So track your starts. Measure success by starts. Measure failure by inaction. Make starting the one metric you use to evaluate performance and progress. Ask yourself: "Am I making a genuine effort?" If so, your performance is beyond reproach. Ask yourself: "Do I return often to my task, with less hesitation and more confidence?" If so, you are making great progress.

When you truly commit to persistent starting (making an effort, again and again) as your one metric for performance, you will gain access to a deep well of patience and determination. The next step is to take pressure off other results, giving them room to breathe and grow.

STOP WORRYING ABOUT EVERYTHING ELSE

You won't find it difficult to congratulate yourself for getting started. It's attractive to measure success by starts, because it means that every effort is an automatic victory. But to allow starting to truly guide your efforts is not easy. You will still be tempted to chase external results. As long as results (which you can never control) dominate your self evaluation, any attention you might give to starting is an empty gesture. To really put your faith in starting, you must be willing to accept everything else as it is, at least for now.

You must remain unimpressed by any gains you make, and proceed in spite of the disappointments you suffer. A focus on starting requires a *neutral acceptance* of exactly the things most people obsess over—sales made, miles run, words written, links clicked, widgets built. Worrying about those things probably caused a majority of your past failures, and they will destroy you again if you rely on them.

Suppose you are overweight. There is little doubt that if you ran as far as you could, every other day for six months, your health and physique would improve. Doing something so obviously useful for half a year would guarantee meaningful progress. You might even lose a few pounds in the first week. Success! But if you're watching the scale every day, judging yourself by what appears, you definitely won't last six months. When you gain back those three pounds in week four, you will become discouraged and quit.

Never mind that the extra weight is probably new muscle. Never mind that in those four weeks you've gained more energy, become more athletic, and strengthened your heart. When you tie your confidence to daily results, every up or down requires an explanation and demands an adjustment. You double down on what's working today, and when it falters tomorrow, you abandon it. A fruitful practice cannot develop that way; progress is rarely so linear. Constant tinkering creates painful circles of confusion and doubt, and often leads to chronic quitting.

Of course, you shouldn't *ignore* external results—they are part of reality. It would be foolish to deny the existence of pounds on a scale or sales in a week.

Instead, challenge their significance. Stop charging neutral events with your own emotions. Facts are just facts; only your judgments can make them 'good' or 'bad'. Choose to see them as assurance that things are moving, that interesting changes are taking place. Stop using short-term results as an excuse for quitting in moments of doubt, when you are worried you might fail. Use them instead as essential feedback for steering the engine of persistent action through inevitable periods of weakness.

3. START WITHOUT HESITATION

"Never put off until tomorrow that which can be done the day after tomorrow."

— Mark Twain

THE OPPOSITE OF INITIATIVE

Procrastination is the opposite of initiative. Initiative decides, procrastination analyzes. Initiative starts, procrastination waits. To be more precise, procrastination is the delay between mental commitment (the moment you decide, *I should do this, I'm going to do this*) and physical action.

Procrastination often feels harmless. What's a little delay, anyway? Things take time, right? It's not like you're giving up. You'll get on it tomorrow, first thing. And tomorrow morning, you'll realize it would be *even better* to start next week because you'll be finished with _____ by then and can really focus.

These self deceptions make procrastination possible. In our busy lives, putting something off can *always* be rationalized and justified. There's nothing easier, and that's bad news. Because procrastination isn't harmless at all.

PROCRASTINATION THREATENS THE START

All moments are not created equal. Imagine letting go of a balloon outside. There are just a few seconds when you can jump and grasp the string, and then it's gone. It's moving slowly, but you won't reach it. You missed your chance.

Opportunities for action, too, begin floating away when you don't seize them in the early moments. When you hesitate and delay, you are not just pushing something back. Procrastination makes it less likely that you will actually start.

This is a logical result. If you can wait a day, you can wait two days. If you can wait two days, you can wait a week. After a week, you will justify your failure to act. Maybe it wasn't that important. You'll have better ideas. Life goes on, and your opportunity is gone with it. The timetable may vary depending on the activity, but the process doesn't change.

Anything that threatens starting is kryptonite to your productivity.

PROCRASTINATION CONSUMES ENERGY AND SAPS MOTIVATION

"...and already I felt the death loneliness that comes at the end of every day that is wasted in your life." — Ernest Hemingway, *A Moveable Feast*

Even if you succeed in overcoming procrastination and finally get started, you've already paid a steep price. First, of course, there is the wasted time—you will never get it back. The damage you inflict on energy and morale, however, are the true costs of procrastination. Everyone has put things off before, and everyone has experienced the same nagging, draining sensation it brings.

Procrastination consumes *real energy*. The moment you make a mental commitment to doing something, you tap into the well of energy required to complete your task. You continue to consume that energy until you've made good on your commitment. It's like leaving your headlights on. Whether you use the energy or not, it's being consumed.

If you do your work, energy is consumed by action, concentration and the satisfaction of a job well done. If you don't, energy is consumed by guilt, distraction and anxiety. Procrastination isn't free, and many of us have experienced Hemingway's "death loneliness", the price of wasted opportunity.

Just as forgotten headlights drain your car's battery, which can prevent it from starting, procrastination also saps the motivation needed to make your next start. Procrastination creates a cycle of discouragement and inaction. You haven't done anything, which makes you feel bad about yourself, and when you feel bad about yourself, you don't feel like doing anything.

START WITHOUT HESITATION

We just established that a delayed start is *not* just as good as a timely one—a delayed start comes with all the baggage of procrastination. Also recall that getting started is the most difficult part of doing, and it becomes clear how starting without hesitation represents a huge advantage in getting things done.

Starting without hesitation means starting immediately at the first good opportunity. Let's say you decide to bake a cake after work. When you reach home, don't turn on the TV; don't use the bathroom or feed your dog. Don't even pet your dog. Baking that cake should be the very first thing you do after setting down your keys. That's what it means to start without hesitation.

If it sounds extreme, then you've understood correctly. To start what needs starting, *now* and without distraction or delay, is indeed a rare behavior. It's wasting time on 100 little things that is totally normal, perfectly average. Consider the habits of all the people you know. Being consistently bold and decisive is not normal. Someone who doesn't hesitate is truly exceptional.

STRENGTHEN YOUR DECIDE-ACT LOOP

Everything you do requires two steps: 1) decision and 2) action. Over the course of a day, you execute this decide-act loop dozens of times as you carry out decisions and make new ones. If you become conscious of this process and work to strengthen it, starting things without hesitation will become painless. You must *unlearn* indecision and hesitation through daily practice, the same way you learned them.

Practice these three behaviors to strengthen your decide-act loop and make starting easier.

1. Practice making decisions with confidence.

Napoleon Hill wrote that "indecision and procrastination are twin brothers." When you're bad at making up your mind, you live in a swamp of uncertainty and delay. It's nearly impossible for someone who isn't decisive to be effective at taking action, and every decision counts. How much time have you spent picking out your clothes in the morning or debating where to eat dinner? You get good at what you practice, and chronic indecisiveness leads to chronic hesitation.

Practice making decisions, even small ones—*especially* small ones—with confidence and purpose. Observe yourself during the process, and repeat your intentions: *I'm going to make a clear decision, without wasting time.* Pride yourself on being decisive, and look for opportunities to exercise your power to choose. In a group, offer to pick the restaurant. At work, offer to schedule the meeting. People won't think you're bossy or self-absorbed. They'll be impressed and relieved that someone is finally willing to decide with confidence.

A good decision settles all the critical details and leaves nothing to be decided later on. A good decision results in a specific commitment. Observe how the following decisions improve as they move from vague to specific, from ambiguous to actionable.

I'm going to start exercising.
I'm going to start running.
I'm going to start running this week.
I'm going for a run this Wednesday.
I'm going for a run this Wednesday at 7 a.m.

2. Follow through on your decisions.

Have you ever suffered because of an unreliable friend? They swear they're coming, and cancel at the last minute. They promise to help, but bail out with an excuse. Eventually you just give up. You realize there is no point in inviting them; it's not worth the frustration or the bad feelings.

Every time you bail out on a made decision, you betray yourself. Like the promises of an unreliable friend, you come to learn that your choices are not to be trusted. If you fail yourself over and over, eventually you just give up. That's why it's so important to follow through on the decisions you make.

Do not reverse or change a decision unless it's unavoidable. If you said you'll run, run. If you decide to watch a particular movie, buy the ticket and go. If you decided to take a nap but now you're not feeling tired, lay down and close your eyes for 10 minutes. Will your life fall apart without such extreme enforcement? No, but keep in mind that each time you make an exception, you weaken your resolve. Deliberate exaggeration helps to minimize those exceptions.

Even when circumstances spoil your plans, do not abandon a decision. Instead, make sure every decision is consummated with *some* action. Your effort doesn't need to be perfect; it's the follow-through that matters.

If Wednesday morning arrives and you're not

feeling well, take a short walk to avoid abandoning your commitment to exercise. If you're too ill to leave the house, take that walk or run the first moment you are able. No matter what it takes, match every decision with an action to close the loop. When you always follow through, your decisions carry weight, and you earn your own trust.

3. *Minimize the time between decision and action.*

Tighten the link between decision and action by following through with speed. Note how long it takes to get started, and work to reduce or eliminate delay. Try to make the loop compact and efficient: Decide. Act. Decide. Act. Decide. Act.

When action follows immediately after decision, there is no time for circumstances to change or sabotage your plans. Reducing the time between decision and action also makes starting easier.

Like a drafting race car benefits from lower pressure and drag, an action that follows close behind a decision takes advantage of the momentum it creates.

CREATE A ROUTINE FOR STARTING

Think of a good routine as an on-ramp for starting. Once you've entered the routine, you're less likely to stop or turn around. It carries you right into your work. Here's my starting routine for writing:

1. <u>Close all programs</u> on my computer.
2. <u>Run a cleaner</u> that wipes the computer's short term memory and removes temporary junk; a digital clean slate.
3. While the cleaning software works, I find some <u>coffee or soda</u>.
4. <u>Clear my workspace</u> (typically my desk and office) of unnecessary items, leaving only notebook, pen, coffee and computer.
5. Put my phone in <u>airplane mode</u> so I won't be distracted/disturbed.
6. <u>Shut the door</u>. (or put on headphones if I'm outside my office).

7. <u>Open the file</u> that I'm using.
8. Write down a <u>start time</u>.
9. <u>Write one complete sentence</u> in the section I'm working on.

The entire process takes less than five minutes, but following these nine steps really locks me into what I'm about to do. The routine tells my subconscious, *it's time to create*. Routines work because they reduce the number of choices you need to make, generate a desired mental state, and automate the process of starting. Create a routine for whatever you're working on and follow the steps each time you start. An effective starting routine should be:

Short and simple: includes only necessary steps (those needed to get you started).
Consistent: follows a fixed sequence that can be internalized and repeated.
Put into writing: forces you to be clear and specific; someone else could follow it if they wanted to.

Portable: not tied to a specific location or context.
Independent: doesn't rely on the availability or cooperation of anything/anyone else.
Complete: ends in something real.

This last feature, completeness, deserves a little explanation. The last step of your starting routine should be the first step of your actual work. For me, completing a sentence means I've definitely begun writing. That sentence carries me over a threshold; even if I stopped there, I could say that I wrote something, that I made a real start.

For the programmer, a real start may be 15 lines of code. For the painter, paint squeezed from the tube onto the palette, or the first brushstroke. Figure out what qualifies as a real start for you, and make it the last step of your routine.

Warning: do not confuse routines with rules. *Rules* about starting (*I am going to do yoga on Mondays; I'm always going to eat breakfast before I paint*) often turn into excuses for not starting (*I can't go to yoga with you—it's not my day; I couldn't paint because I skipped breakfast).*

4. PRACTICE SMALL ACTION

"All difficult things have their origin in that which is easy, and great things in that which is small."

— Lao Tzu

IMITATING WILLPOWER

You likely know from experience that the *mental* challenges of persistence can be far greater than the physical ones. It follows, then, that building and using initiative requires an amount of willpower.

But what is willpower? When they hear the word, many people imagine gritted teeth and cold-blooded determination; long hours and not letting up; self-denial and self-sacrifice; enduring the unenjoyable to earn a future payout. Those are all *fantasy* conceptions of willpower, the kind of willpower shown in movies—Rocky Balboa running past burning trash cans and punching carcasses in a meat locker as a chorus wails, *"Trying hard now…it's so hard now."*

Our imitations of fantasy willpower do more harm than good. Sometimes under a tight deadline you do have to toil without rest and be a bit miserable. But that kind of struggle is unsustainable, and it certainly won't help you build initiative, which is a *sustained* desire and ability to get started. Imitation willpower only leads to burnout and discouragement.

Real willpower is not a form of endurance or self-denial. Real willpower comes from enjoyment and satisfaction, not from suffering. It is the glad *willingness* to keep going, to eagerly do what needs doing. So whatever makes working more enjoyable increases willpower, the mental strength to carry out your plans. Instead of imitating willpower, you can develop real willpower by practicing small action.

PRACTICE SMALL ACTION

"The smallest deed is better than the greatest intention." — John Burroughs

Small action is a short burst of focused, useful effort. Small action works because it is aligned with our human physiology. Our capacity for intense effort—even mental effort—is *physically* limited. We are not built like the computers and other machines we use. We are not designed to run all day and night, without pause or recovery. Our energy must be used and renewed in continuous cycles of expenditure and rest.

Small action leads to better work. You can produce more with 30 minutes of high-energy, focused effort than several hours of disengaged clock-watching. Small action is also *flexible*; it results in lots of attempts, iterations, and a steady stream of feedback. From Crossfit training to "agile" computer programming and *kaizen* production methods, versions of small action have become best practices in many fields.

We're going to use small action to build initiative and boost willpower. Working in short bursts ensures many opportunities to practice starting again. It's also a way to build momentum without risking burnout or overload. Think of small action as a purposefully contained effort; that means stopping well is as important as starting well. The peace of mind that comes with a good effort followed by a clean break makes working comfortable, and work that feels good generates plenty of willpower.

You need just three simple rules to master small action:

1. Set minimums and maximums
2. Give a quality effort
3. Stop with pleasure

MINIMUMS AND MAXIMUMS

Each time you start something, set a minimum and maximum for your session. Make a tiny commitment to do something real, and promise to quit when you reach a certain point, no matter what.

***Make a tiny commitment** (**set a minimum**)*. Commit to five push-ups, one sales call or 10 minutes of painting. For writing, I usually set my minimum at 50 words if I already know what I'm going to write, and 30 *minutes* if I don't. When I'm facing a deadline, the minimum is much higher. Choose a unit of measurement and a level of effort that makes sense, and always err on the side of less.

Your minimum should be a standard based on quantity and effort rather than quality or performance. *Shoot 100 free throws* is a good minimum. *Make 100 free throws* is not. A good minimum invites you in for an easy score, and makes starting attractive. There's no pressure. Just do this little bit. It's "just the tip" productivity. Even a single, symbolic brushstroke, sentence or sit-up is progress.

Of course, once you finish a sales call or write 50 words, it's unlikely you'll stop there. Everybody knows it's never just the tip. Because you really *do* want to write that novel. You *do* want to ace your exam. You *do* want to start a business or finally get in shape.

The things most important to us are often the hardest to work on, because they come loaded down with our expectations, hopes and fears. A minimum is nothing more than a friendly shove into the cold pool. If you can just *get started*, most of the time you will warm up, settle in, and get something meaningful done.

***Promise to quit** (**set a maximum**)*. A maximum establishes the upper limit of what you're about to do. It keeps you firmly in control of the experience, and gives you something to look forward to—stopping. A maximum is a promise to quit, and quitting is a promise you can keep.

I often set myself a range of 50-600 words. I commit to writing at least 50 words, and I promise to stop no matter what if I hit 600. If you don't set a limit, your victories can easily turn into defeats. Energetic, ambitious people often sabotage their goals by trying to do too much, too fast.

Suppose you've begun a strength training regimen. Because you're a novice, getting into the gym can be intimidating. So you set a minimum—*one set on the bench-press and I can leave*. You finish one set, and then a second. It feels great. You could leave, satisfied that you doubled up on your commitment. But you're rolling now, so you decide to go for eight sets.

By the seventh set, your technique has deteriorated as you struggle to complete the reps. You suddenly feel a sharp twinge in your back, and the bar drops to your chest. Someone nearby helps you from under the weight and out to your car. The experience is humiliating. You wonder why you even came.

Pushing too hard in anything will result in burnout, failure and discouragement. If I sit too long at my computer, I start to do less writing and more criticizing. After a certain point, I will invariably conclude that what I'm writing is no good, and that puts me in a bad mood.

Trying to do too much only makes your next start harder. Once you've depleted your energy and focus, it's time to stop. Setting a maximum will make starting easier, but it also ensures that you quit while you're ahead, locking in well-deserved gains. Together, minimums and maximums turn starting into a productive, satisfying experience, one you're more likely to repeat.

GIVE A QUALITY EFFORT

The comfort and certainty of working within a minimum/maximum range will boost the quality of your work. Because you know only a modest effort is required before you can rest, it's easier to focus and make the most of your minutes. Here are some tips to further maximize the productivity of your small action.

Shut off distractions. Remember that your starting routine should include steps to establish the right environment for your task. Turn off electronic distractions and anticipate/neutralize other interruptions before you start.

Do one thing. Pick a single, specific task to focus on for each start. If I commit to writing for one hour, I won't switch back and forth between research and writing during that time, even though research supports my writing. I'll break them into separate starts so I can give my best attention to each.

Stay on task. If you decide to practice the piano for 30 minutes, don't pause the clock and run to the grocery store after 15 minutes. Make a decision to work, start promptly, and stick with it until you reach your minimum. If you find that process to be a burden, then set a lower minimum.

Don't rush. Small action doesn't mean careless or frantic work. You are working to become comfortable with starting early and often, and you'll start again soon. There is no great hurry to produce in any one session. Practice working at a comfortable pace.

STOP WITH INTENTION, STOP WITH PLEASURE

Stopping well is critical to your success with small action. You should stop with intention, just as you started. And you should feel damn good about it. Here is how to master the small action stop:

Stop when you lose focus. If you've satisfied your minimum but haven't yet reached your maximum, when should you stop? Stop when your mind starts to wander or your interest in the task fades. Concentration is what separates small action from mindless toil and wasted energy.

Stop where you can start again easily. If you're working well and staying engaged, then stop where you can start again easily. Quitting when you're frustrated or unsure of what to do makes the next start less appealing. Instead, stop while you've still got momentum. Hemingway used this method to avoid writer's block. He advised: "The best way is always to stop when you are going good and when you know what will happen next. If you do that every day... you will never be stuck."

Make it official. Remember the format I suggested for tracking your starts? I always record my STOP time, too, because it forces me to be definite about stopping. I also use a shutdown routine to make sure my activities don't bleed into one another. I put my computer to sleep, turn off the lights and close the office door behind me. Going through these motions adds a pleasing finality to stopping. Even if I'm coming back to work again shortly, I like to shut down and spend a few minutes in satisfaction at having done my work. You should too. You've earned it.

Stop with pleasure. Even if you quit the moment you reach your minimum, always quit with pride and satisfaction. Even if you performed poorly, *stop with pleasure.* You did exactly what you said you would. You made a plan to do useful work and you followed through by making an effort. You know you can do it again. No matter how small your action, you should always walk away in full triumph.

5. START AGAIN, RELENTLESSLY

"The day you decide to do it is your lucky day."

— Japanese proverb

BE RELENTLESS

Persistent action resembles the steady, quiet power of the ocean tide. Each wave erodes another obstacle and claims a tiny piece of the coast. Over time, nothing can hold back the tide.

And like the tide, the force of persistent action is cumulative—with enough starts, you will wear down and overwhelm the obstacles between you and your goals. You will eliminate failures of action, and the momentum of your relentless pursuit will carry you past many external challenges, too.

There is no surprise twist or contrarian advice in this last section on how to build initiative. You've considered the power of action and initiative, you've heard why starting deserves your focus, you've learned how to make starting easier and more enjoyable, and now… it's time to execute.

Like any skill, initiative must be mastered through concentrated practice and plenty of repetition. Initiative is mastered by starting and stopping and starting again. And then again a thousand times.

EXAGGERATE EARLY ON

While you're still getting used to the feel of attacking a goal in a large number of short bursts, you should exaggerate the process. Take it too far. Make it ridiculous. For example, if you can devote three hours to your task, split that time up into as many starts as you can. Follow your routines for starting and stopping without omission; go through all the motions. Here is an entry from my early days of practicing initiative.

START 2:15
STOP 2:20
START 2:31
STOP 2:37
START 2:44
STOP 2:57
START 3:08
STOP 3:19
START 3:25

STOP 3:30
START 3:40
STOP 3:45
START 4:00
STOP 4:11
START 4:22
STOP 4:30
START 5:00
STOP 5:15

Instead of sitting at my computer from 2:15 to 5:15, I broke the afternoon's work into nine separate starts averaging 11 minutes each. And every time, I went through my whole routine (wiping the memory before starting, closing the computer and shutting my office after each stop, etc.).

I'll admit that I sometimes grew impatient waiting for the various programs to load again and again. But exaggerating the number of times I started made a tremendous difference in my writing. It was so useful that I worked that way for weeks, generating lots of new ideas in 10-minute bursts.

Before I articulated my ideas about initiative and the importance of starting, writing was often uncomfortable for me, and my output was inconsistent. I would sit down to write when I had an idea. After exhausting the thread, I would remain for hours trying to come up with more.

That's what a good writer would do, right? Stay on the job. After four or five hours with little production, I felt terrible. Those sessions created a good deal of anxiety and doubt, and I came to dread the process of writing. I would look for any excuse not to sit down and start.

But when I began to practice persistent starting, my creativity and productivity soared. I stopped worrying about whether my writing was any good, and instead focused on *doing it* with a cartoon-like persistence. I sat down to write even when I had nothing interesting to say. It was doing for doing's sake, and it worked beautifully.

In the afternoon charted above, I wrote 1,400 words, and some of it was pretty good. Taking lots of short breaks gave my mind space to work without expectation, and I usually went back to the computer with something more to add.

Deliberately exaggerating the number of times I started quickly wore down all the emotional resistance I had come to associate with writing. Through sheer volume and frequency of exposure, I broke and tamed writing. I stopped fearing it and started owning it. Writing became natural and enjoyable again. And relentless starting is still the sole focus of my work habits. I wrote this book in hundreds of short bursts. I never feel bad about stopping, because it gives me another chance to start.

You might wonder whether exaggerated starting is impractical outside of my writing example. You might be thinking, *so basically this guy is pacing around for hours, and sits down every few minutes to write a little bit*. There's some truth to that, but the strength of my practice comes from being deliberate. I have used the same techniques to destroy resistance and build initiative in many contexts.

When I was trying to pick up running, for example, I made sure to exaggerate my starts. In one weekend I ran nine different times. Each time I would shower and change back into my normal clothes. A few times I only waited an hour before starting the process all over, changing and going outside, running, showering, and changing again.

I don't know whether that was ideal from a fitness standpoint, and all the showering did dry my skin a bit, but exaggerating definitely made starting easier. With all those repetitions under my belt, I didn't hesitate the next week when I was busy and didn't feel like running. I had developed a solid base of initiative and some good momentum.

BE AN OPPORTUNIST
(START WHEN YOU CAN AND WILL)

Don't worry too much about finding ideal moments to make your starts; you're just as likely to blow them off as any other moment. In my life, I've already wasted plenty of 'perfect' opportunities, and I'm not alone. Everyone I know has thrown away great chances to get something done. And everyone I know has delivered under the ugliest of circumstances, too.

If you want or need something badly enough, you can always find a way. And if it's just not that important, you can always find an excuse. So it puzzles me when I see someone spending lots of energy trying to create the perfect circumstances, as if the right situation will do the work of starting for them.

Trying to control circumstances, or fighting

against them, is a fool's errand. It's like a pilot trying to control the weather instead of the plane.

Instead, strive to be a genuine opportunist, someone who spends less time grading opportunities and more time seizing them—even the ugly ones. You cannot be relentless and picky at the same time. So stop thinking about when you *should* do something or when you'd *prefer* to do it, and instead focus on when you *can* and *will* do it.

Maybe you harbor a vision of yourself writing poetry at home on the weekends, but you never really get around to it. You sometimes find yourself sketching the poems on your lunch break at work, imagining how glorious they'll be when you write them 'for real' in the solitude of your favorite space.

Guess what? You are a lunch break poet. Seize your opportunities with gratitude and energy, and make the most of them, even when they don't match a romantic vision of how you're going to reach your goal.

START WHEN YOUR HEART ISN'T IN IT

―――――――――

Sex with love (making love) and sex without love are externally indistinguishable. What I'm saying is, you don't need to wait for inspiration to strike to make a start. Make a start even when your heart isn't in it. Do it *especially* when your heart isn't in it, because that's when starting is hardest. Nobody has trouble starting when they're all fired up.

Acting in spite of your own frustration, boredom or indifference shows real initiative.

TRY TO START ON EVERY DATE

It's a great practice to make a start every day, and you're more likely to succeed if focus on starting every *date*.

Have you ever been in a bar with a sign that says "Free Beer Tomorrow"? Tomorrow gets pushed back every morning at sunrise; tomorrow never comes.

It's also true that *every day* is today. You can indefinitely put off a promise to do something 'today'. But *dates* are unique. You only get one January 1st, March 10th and June 5th per year. If you miss them, they're gone.

Use calendar entries to track your starts, and think in dates instead of days. And remember that earlier is usually better. When you push your starts back later in the day, they're less likely to happen. Unexpected demands, excuses, fatigue and other saboteurs tend to accumulate as the day wears on.

6. ADOPT ACTION AS A VALUE

"Whatever we put our attention on grows stronger in our life; whatever we take our attention away from withers and disappears."

— Deepak Chopra, *The Seven Spiritual Laws of Success*

THE POWER OF VALUES

"Your values become your destiny." — Mahatma Gandhi

Adopting action as a value will bolster your efforts to build initiative and become an effective starter. Cherished values are powerful moderators of our behavior. They guide us toward certain choices and away from others. Values can hold the line where logic, technique, experience, preparation and everything else might fail.

Suppose you have to take a business trip with an attractive coworker who has come on to you before. And oops, you're married. What is it that keeps you from misbehaving? You could make a list of techniques and rules, and try to optimize the situation. (*Get a room in a different hotel; don't have more than two drinks at dinner; redirect conversation to the topic of your wonderful spouse, etc.*).

Those methods are sensible enough, but if you lack the *values* to support them, no amount of logic or planning can guarantee the proper behavior. Armed with the same cheat sheet, however, someone who *also* possesses strong values like *commitment, love, honesty* and *fidelity* is far more likely to do the right thing at the moment of truth. That is the power of values.

And what about action? Part One explained why action deserves your highest esteem. To review: Action and progress are the motive forces of the entire universe. Action is the one indispensable element of success; in the struggle to become your highest self, action is a matter of life or death.

By infusing action with the significance of principle, by making it a value, you reinforce the practical with the spiritual. As a value, action will acquire an extra purpose beyond the attainment of your objectives. Concentrated effort comes to represent much more than a means to an end. And both of those changes will help you execute on all the methods taught in this book. So how do you do it? Practice, of course. The following practices will help build your conviction in action as a value:

ACTION CONSCIOUSNESS
(GO DEAF TO THE NOISE)

Practice viewing life through the filter of action. See the world as a place where things either are or are not getting done. Pretend everything that isn't action is just noise, a distraction to be filtered out and ignored. Specifically, refuse to be impressed by any of the following:

Promises
Excuses
Hopes
Interpretations
Rationales
Predictions
Doubts
Beliefs
Worries
Complaints
Wishes
Justifications

Practicing action-consciousness for a few weeks will help you see that many of those things *really are just noise*. They rarely make anything better or worse; they lack the substance required to have an impact.

You can suffer from chronic doubt and still achieve greatly. You can also waste a life full of belief. In the end, what you actually do (or don't do) will largely determine the course of your life. So ignore every excuse and promise from yourself and others. Go deaf to the noise and you will see clearly the direction anyone is headed, by listening to actions.

BE ZEALOUS

To the zealot, nothing is a mystery. Every question has a single, satisfactory answer. A zealot is somebody with a very narrow worldview. You find them most often in religion and politics. To the zealot of religion, nothing happens which is not part of the Divine Scheme. Likewise, the political zealot molds every fact and circumstance into proof for the cause. Zealous single-mindedness is incredibly effective for reinforcing values.

So practice being a zealot of action. Try to explain everything in terms of action. Try to see how action—what's not being done or what's being done and how—is both the question and the answer to everything. Of course, the truth might not be so absolute. But action-is-everything zeal comes closer to the truth than anything else.

THINK IN VALUES

Start to recognize values in your daily efforts. If you think of going for a run as a demonstration of your initiative (instead of seeing it as just exercise), it will be easier to follow through. Tying tasks to values give the tasks a much greater significance. Values can make even menial or thankless tasks attractive. Cleaning dishes in a soup kitchen can be a happy task when it is experienced as an expression of *service* and *charity*.

And this is no mental hack—it's the truth. Going running when you said you would *is* an expression of action and proof of initiative. Serving in a soup kitchen *is* an act of charity. Adjust your perception and take some emotional credit. You should feel good about yourself every time you live out your values.

You can also use values as a guide and a rubric for your activities. Look back over your day, remember what you did and how you spent your hours. If someone else had watched you all day, would they say that you're a person who clearly values action, who takes initiative? If you study how and where your behaviors and values are out of harmony, you can slowly work to close the gap between them, one start at a time.

THE END

———————

It's time to turn your belly fire into steam and make it go. I hope you find many opportunities to take action and bring some more happiness into your life. Best of luck, and may your progress be *startacular.*

ABOUT THE AUTHOR

Daniel Zoller is a professor of international business, author and speaker.

Read more online at danielzoller.net

www.ingramcontent.com/pod-product-compliance
Lightning Source LLC
Chambersburg PA
CBHW031448040426
42444CB00007B/1023